Aberdeenshire
COUNCIL

Aberdeenshire Libraries
www.aberdeenshire.gov.uk/libraries
Renewals Hotline 01224 661511

2 9 NOV 2016

HQ

2 8 DEC 2017

Pebble® Plus

Cats, Cats, Cats

Cat Care

by Christina Mia Gardeski

raintree

a Capstone company — publishers for children

Raintree is an imprint of Capstone Global Library Limited, a company incorporated in England and Wales having its registered office at 264 Banbury Road, Oxford, OX2 7DY – Registered company number: 6695582

www.raintree.co.uk
myorders@raintree.co.uk

ISBN 978 1 4747 2261 2
20 19 18 17 16
10 9 8 7 6 5 4 3 2 1

British Library Cataloguing in Publication Data
A full catalogue record for this book is available from the British Library.

Editorial Credits
Jaclyn Jaycox, editor; Philippa Jenkins, designer;
Pam Mitsakos, media researcher; Steve Walker, production specialist

Photo Credits
Alamy: Juniors Bildarchiv GmbH, 9; Capstone Press, Dan Nunn, 1; Getty Images: Arthur Tilley, 5; Shutterstock: ajlatan, 17, Alexey Kozhemyakin, 11, g215, 7, Jakub Zak, cover, Jeanine Brouwer, 3, back cover, Milles Studio, 21, red rose, design element throughout, Stanimir G.Stoev, 19, tarapong srichaiyos, 15, Yimmyphotography, 13

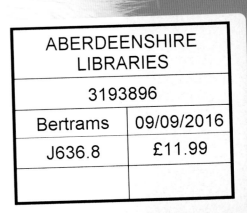

Every effort has been made to contact copyright holders of material reproduced in this book. Any omissions will be rectified in subsequent printings if notice is given to the publisher.

All the Internet addresses (URLs) given in this book were valid at the time of going to press. However, due to the dynamic nature of the Internet, some addresses may have changed, or sites may have changed or ceased to exist since publication. While the author and publisher regret any inconvenience this may cause readers, no responsibility for any such changes can be accepted by either the author or the publisher.

Printed and bound in China.

Contents

Cat care

It may seem that cats can care for themselves. But cats have lived with people for thousands of years. Pet cats trust their owners to take care of them.

Healthy food

Cats need healthy food. Protein
keeps them strong. Cats get protein
from meat in wet or dry cat food.
Foods we eat such as milk and
onions can make cats ill.

Fresh water

Cats need fresh water.

Put out a clean bowl of fresh water every day. Many cats enjoy drinking from a pet water fountain.

Time to play

Playing is one way for your cat to get exercise. Some cats like to bat balls or pounce on paper bags. Play with your cat as much as you can.

Claw care

A cat's claws need to be kept trim.

Cats need to scratch. They scratch to

peel off the dead outer layer of their

claws. You can give your cat a

scratching post.

Good grooming

Cats lick themselves to stay clean.

But you can help with grooming.

Brush your cat to keep it from

getting fur balls. Most cats only

need baths if they are very dirty.

Clean litter

Kittens and indoor cats need clean litter trays. Scoop out dirty litter every day. Empty and clean the tray every week. Dirty litter can make cats ill.

Indoor cats

Most cats go outside to hunt and play in the garden. People who don't have gardens may keep their cats indoors. Indoor cats enjoy spending time with their owners.

A check-up

Cats need check-ups once a year. The vet checks the cat's eyes, ears and mouth. They listen to its heart and lungs. Check-ups will help you to keep your cat healthy.

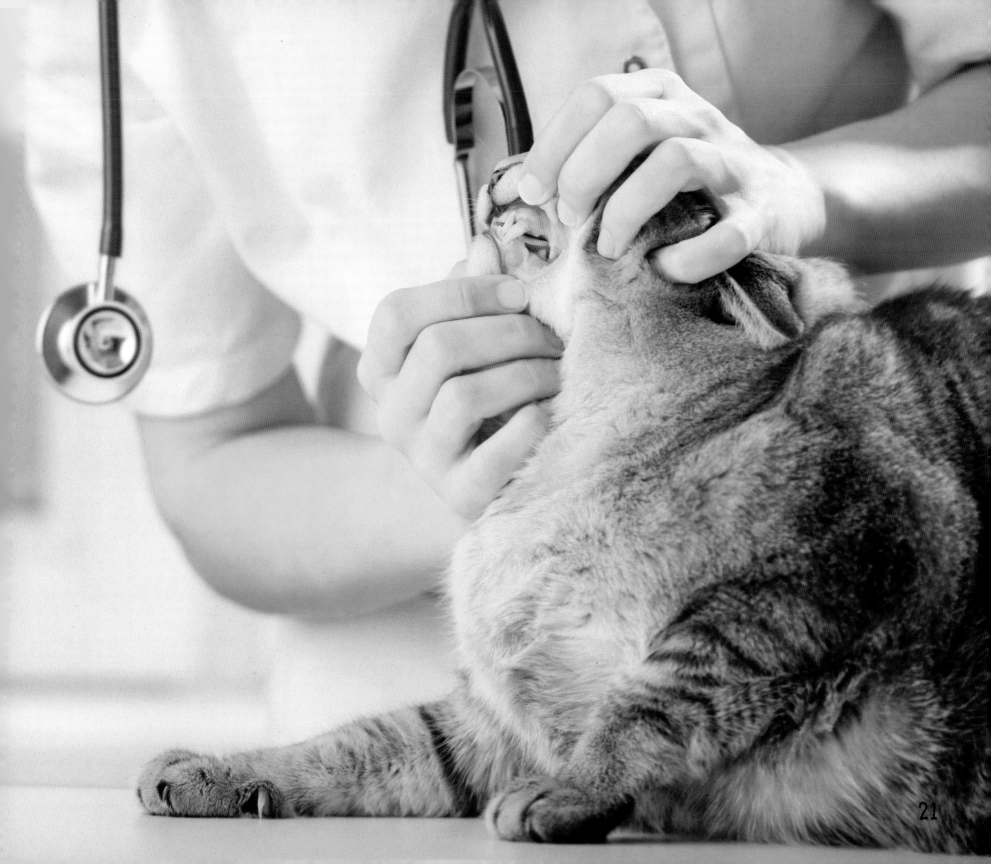

Glossary

exercise   moving the body to become strong and healthy

fur ball   ball of fur that forms in a cat's stomach after it has licked itself clean

groom   keep clean

litter tray   tray filled with small bits of wood, paper or clay where cats go to the toilet

pounce   jump on something suddenly and grab it

protein   part of food that builds strong bones and muscles

vet   person who takes care of animals

Read more

First Book of Cats, Isabel Thomas (A&C Black Childrens & Educational, 2014)

Kitty's Guide to Caring for Your Cat (Pets' Guides), Anita Ganeri (Raintree, 2013)

Looking after Cats and Kittens, Katherine Starke (Usborne Publishing Ltd, 2013)

Websites

www.cats.org.uk/cats-for-kids

Discover even more about cats! Read articles, watch videos and play games to learn all about cats and how to care for them.

www.rspca.org.uk/adviceandwelfare/pets/cats

Find out more about owning a cat.

Comprehension questions

- Describe one way you can help your cat with its grooming.

- Caring for a cat is a big job. What do you think is the hardest part?

- How often should you take your cat to the vet for a check-up? Why is it important?

Index